Beloved Brother, Beloved Sister
Poems for Palestine

Kevin Hadduck

Fomite
Burlington, VT

ISBN-13: 978-1-959984-18-4
Library of Congress Control Number: 2023944483

Fomite
58 Peru Street
Burlington, VT 05401
www.fomitepress.com

08-21-2023

"Poetry and beauty are always making peace. When you read something beautiful you find coexistence; it breaks walls down."

—Mahmoud Darwish

Contents

Dedication

My gratitude for the inspiration that led to these poems belongs first to Doaa Mohaisen, a student on scholarship from Gaza, Palestine, whom I met one day in early September of 2016. Doaa came into my office at Carroll College, seeking the help of a tutor for Linguistics and Latin. Over time, we became friends, and I found in Doaa a brilliant mind, a beautiful heart, and a playful spirit. My wife Linda and I took her on road trips and hikes here in Montana, where the sparse population and enormous expanses of nearly empty land contrasted sharply with the desperately crowded and constrained Gaza Strip. Nonetheless, I told Doaa, "I love this irony, that while I live in a huge, wide-open space in a wealthy country and you in such a small, cramped, and impoverished place, you have made my world so much larger and my heart so much richer." To all of my Palestinian friends, and to others whom I have come to know along the way, I say the same.

Most of the friends named in this book are Palestinian and live in Gaza, Palestine or have recently moved from Gaza to other countries (Qatar, UAE, Canada, Belgium, Italy, Portugal, England, Turkey, Australia). Several live in Lebanon. A few friends named herein are not Palestinian, but Syrian, Jordanian, Israeli, and American. They have expressed a deep sympathy for the Palestinian struggle for freedom, civil rights, and dignity.

I owe a forever debt of gratitude to friends in We Are Not Numbers (www.wearenotnumbers.org), a Gazan organization mentoring young Palestinian writers in English and telling their stories to a Western audience. Many others in Gaza have blessed me with their friendship.

I cannot, nor will I ever, find words numerous enough or beautiful enough to say what beauty and joy these friends have brought to me. They are among the kindest, gentlest, and most uplifting people I have ever known. "Your existence is beautiful; you are a beautiful gift from Allah," I tell them. I write these poems for them, merely to say, "Thank you. I love you."

—Kevin Hadduck

Introductions

From Basman, Gaza

Unfortunately, I have not yet met Kevin in person, yet I see him through his words. We sit on the beach together. We cry and laugh over the darkness. We enjoy the taste of Maklouba together through his poems. He said to me in one of his poems, "Allow me to sit in the sunshine of a street café and taste the dark honey of your laughter, my brothers."

As Pink says in one of her songs, "God, it hurts to be human, but I've got you." I can say to Kevin thank you for your beautiful and honest poems and for your existence in all our lives. You make me not only a better writer, but also a better person. There is nothing like the gift of love that we share. Much love to you.

From Doaa, Gaza/Qatar

In fall 2016, I left the Gaza Strip for the first time in my life to enroll at Carroll College, Helena, Montana as an exchange student. I was scared, but bursting with excitement while traveling alone for the first time. When I needed help with my Latin, I headed to Kevin's office, the Academic Resource Center. Stuffed animals filled the office. A tall, broad-shouldered man with white hair, almost bald, invited me in with a huge smile. We chatted, and later he invited me to join him and his wife on a hike. The day I left the US, I held Kevidello, a stuffed-animal armadillo, which Kevin gifted me. I cried as I hugged Kevin and went to catch my plane. Kevin and I stayed in touch, even after I went back to the Gaza Strip; I taught him some Arabic, which he used in his poems, some of which he wrote to me. Through our correspondence, we learned from each other, and the age and cultural gaps between us seemed to melt away from our friendship that grew day by day. Kevin's circle of Palestinian friends grew, too.

Kevin's poetry is simple, yet profound and shows his flair for people; almost every poem in this book was written about and for a friend, most of them Palestinian.

Kevin gives out a piece of his heart with every poem he writes. He shares the feelings we experience on a day-to-day basis under blockade, impoverishment, and occupation, despite us living worlds apart. In one of his poems, he refers to the Orient/Occident dichotomy in a way emblematic of unity and love, as they both belong to one and the same world. He has an ability to capture Palestinians' dreams, thoughts, blues, and joys and put them in words so eloquent, like music to the ear, in order to show that people from Palestine are just like all human beings.

Ali, Ali, Outs In Free

—for Ali, Gaza

Olly olly oxen free!
Steal your flag and find your tree,
Olive branch and olive leaf,
Pungent fruit and bitter tea.
Ali, Ali, outs in free!

Olly olly oxen free!
Call them all and call them in,
Brother, sister, distant kin.
Hearts left out, now hearts come in.
Ali, Ali, outs in free!

Olly olly oxen free!
All who stay and all who roam,
Journey to your golden dome.
Raise the colors now, you're home.
Ali, Ali, outs in free!

Every One of Us Is One of Us

I want teeming oceans,
deep forested ranges,
not to separate, but to define
us, each one of us a world
of vast seas, duned deserts,
sightless steppes, snowy peaks,
and jungled river valleys.

How we could then revere,
explore in awe each the other
and discover through the years
with every expedition in
that every change of seasons,
every rise and set of sun creates,
as if, a whole new world.

Instead, unawed, one of us kills
one of us and every one of us
is one of us, and two whole worlds
of worlds die unexplored.

If Only You Could See the Bright Flower

—for Huda, Ein el Hilweh

If you could hear, Mariam, I would ask you why
you face only northward? Bright Huda sees you.

She lives just south of you, low in the valley.
Why do you stand so still, silent, serene
on your tower, there on the hill top?
Is Ein el Hilweh no city? Is it no country?

You are comforting the infant in your arms.
It seems you are too busy. How is that, Mariam,
you who understand better than anyone
that your child's light is your light? And so?

Hold my sister Huda, Mariam. She is your child.
The child in your arms, cradled there,
safe against your breast, is every child.
If only you could take her in your arms.

> *"The sun is too hot against my roof,*
> *but I stand here in the valley, looking*
> *to the sea, then up to a statue of Mariam*
> *holding her child, but where is my comfort?"*

Mariam, I would take her in my arms myself,
but I, a stranger, cannot. And who am I?
Mariam, you cannot see your bright daughter.
For all the sunlight there, will you not see her?

I hear that she lives in a dark place, even at noon.
I hear that darkness there blots out the sun.
Mariam, if only you could turn, look southward,
look deep into Ein el Hilweh, into the heart of her

and see the bright lights, the magnificent flowers
of Allah blooming and shining there. See Bright Huda.

A Gift Was Born, September 24

—for Heba A, Gaza/Turkey

Where is the world
to sing in celebration,
sing in joy with Palestine?
Foolish kings, dull of heart,
sigh and tally only numbers:
another birth, another burden.

What good can come from Gaza?
the dull of heart will ask.

While a mother hopes and labors,
and a father bows in fear and joy,
the children dance and sing
who simply love a birth.
Some say Allah Himself
will dance, while angels sing.

What good can come from Gaza?
the dull of heart will ask.

Bring again the chocolates!
Bring knafah, cakes, and pies.
Bring books, new clothes and shoes.
Bring laughter, songs, and stories.
Insha'Allah, the dull, dead world
will hear, will hear! the celebration.

What good is come from Gaza?
those waking hearts may ask.

May all the world rejoice,
as all the world grows rich
by one girl's birth and, oh!
how rich a gift that one girl is.
Now smile and wink at squabbles,
dear Abood; recall her day and sing,

What a gift you you are, dear Heba.
A gift was born. Let all creation sing!

Breathing

—for Basman, Gaza

A spruce needle, one of millions,
green, growing beside my window,
inhales, and in breathing, performs
in near perfection it's vital purpose.

Perched nearby, a western tanager,
flame-breasted in spring plumage,
sings to another.

A magpie, dancing among branches,
paradisal beauty, highland clown,
builds a domed nest.

Bearing witness in this theater,
the leaf exhales, and thus
all the characters breathe.

A small child listening and watching
breathes as the characters of this drama
breathe, without thought.

I reflect beside myself at my window.
They say in Gaza, even children seem old.
The whole world is old and breathless.

Brother, do the tamarisk and olive trees
hold their breath, awaiting catastrophe?
Breathe in. Breathe out. Insh'Allah.
Basman, teach us to breathe like trees.

Breathing

—by Basman, for Kevin

I stand at my open window and breathe.
At dawn, the sun's rays warm my face.
Gaza is silent but for her breathing,
weary from the buzzing of drones.

Another window opens half a world away.
Kevin, I see you standing there, breathing.
Do I breathe the same oxygen here in Gaza?
Do our souls meet with each breath in and out?

The world is clenched in wars, drenched in blood.
Teach them, Kevin, how to let go, how to breathe.

At Her Mirror

—for Sal, Gaza/Abu Dhabi

in gaza
she stands
at her mirror
sending out her voice
no echo returns
all that is seems
to shimmer vanish
as if over hot sand

only one question
remains for her mind

how shall I be

not who not what
as all that defines
has abandoned
her imagination
her grasp on hope

in gaza her voice
wishing to be
a woman evident
undeniable heard
simply heard
sends itself out

her mirror cannot
grant her desire
for simple definition
yet she sees

her shimmering Self
sends out her voice
again remembering
voices that return

testifying to her fullness
her indisputable
power

Riddle for My Sister

—for Doaa, Gaza

My good morning sings
good evening to your ear.
My rising sun uplifts my heart
to hope.
Your setting sun draws you
to reverie.
My shadow leans westward,
yours eastward,
yet you are Orient
and I, Occident.

One sun illuminates us both.
If I search eastward, then,
into my sun that rises,
and you search westward,
into your sun that sets,
do we not see the same vital fire
that inspires both our worlds?
Our worlds are one, then,
not two.

Say I am there, and you are here.
Say we both say, "I am there."

The Grace of You

—for Ghada, Gaza/Doha

Your name, hyada, gada, jhada—
is beautiful to my ears,
slow and untutored as they are.
Say it for me again and then
say it for me again and again,
until my ears master the grace of it.

I cannot find your name in my language,
form your name with my tongue,
or find a place for it to rest in my throat,
but Ghada, I will speak it, blush,
speak it again and again and again,
until my tongue masters the grace of it.

From Doha, Khan Younis, or Gaza City,
I know only pictures, videos like dreams.
Insha'Allah, Insha'Allah, I will know there
the voice of Adhan, the hush of seashore,
voices of Friday Market, and catch there,
in your eyes, the Grace of you.

Bassem at El Bahhar

—for Bassem, Gaza

You dream of coming here, and I, there
to find you in a seaside restaurant.
It would be your smile to catch my eye,
long before your laughter caught my ear,
and oh, the height and breadth of you, brother.
No, I've never been to El Bahhar,
but heard their fiery Zibdyit gambara
will warm the tongue, the cheeks, and heart alike.
But tell me where to find the best maftoul,
the finest Gazan za'atar and taboon bread.
I hear that even restaurants cannot compete
with your finest kitchens. Oh, I am rude, and yet
I will presume upon the greatness of your heart.
Tell me where you live, Bassem! What street?

Love Is that Big

—for Haneen H, Gaza

Your heart, the size of your fist,
keeps rhythm within your chest.

Inside your heart, the echoes
ring through a far greater space.
Planets, stars, nebulae, galaxies,
the whole cosmos pulses like a bell.

If only we would open ourselves
to each other, we would discover
that one heart may contain all hearts.

The mystery is this: Inside your heart,
many people are celebrating together,
singing, dancing, close to each other,
laughing as if drunk, but not on wine.
They have imbibed only love and joy.
They are celebrating. Love is that big.

The Manner of Our Discourse

—for Sal, Gaza/Abu Dhabi

We will eat, you and I, with a chosen guest,
considering the manner of our discourse,
at table spread with platters, bowls, and cups,
baba ganoush, couscous, and maqlouba,
chocolates and kunafa, oranges and dates—

and when we each have rills and rivulets
of mingled juices dripping from our chins,
oil and thick sauce smudging all our faces,
we will eat more, laugh at our indulgence,

until we solve every last problem of the world,
until the child who sat alone and wept
without food or water, without walls,
beneath a small bridge in a dry wahda,
sucks the last sweet jelly from his thumb.

Beauty Asks Herself

—for Huda, Ein El Hilweh

A jet leaves a vanishing trail
across the setting sun.

The sun leaves no lasting glow
among the stars.

The lights of those stars
evanesce within the Milky Way.

Everything passes.
Everything is forgotten.

In Ein El Hilweh, souls pass
along named streets.

Street signs claim,
This is our place to be.

Streets lead to doors
of shops and homes.

In a living room,
beside a small lamp,

a young woman asks herself,
among the billion stars,

Do I matter?
Am I beautiful
to someone?

This Stone and That Wide Ocean

—for Doaa, Gaza

Yes, this stone, this one, and again
the one just there beyond that aspen,
you stepped across, but on that one,
there, with layered rust and gray, you
caught the toe of the boots you borrowed.
And then you ran, laughing, beautiful
in your childlike joy among the pine,
the stately red ponderosa and juniper.

On another trail, through heavy snow,
you stumbled, slid, and fell and rose
and fell again and rose and fell again.
You rejoiced for the ice against your wrists,
the sharp air biting your cheeks, for this
was worship in a new mosque, a new
heaven, and for us, a new voice, welcome
in the choir of our own cathedral.

On this stone, resting like a park bench
beneath the leafless aspen branches,
we sat and talked, the white vapor
of our breath mingling and vanishing.
We spoke of your leaving, the month,
the day, the joy and sorrow of that hour,
our voices merging with the stream
that spilled down to the river valley below.
We did not speak of that wide ocean.

After a Smile from Batoul

—for Batoul, Beirut

I could say that yours
will light a room
shine like the sun
beam from ear to ear
warm a cold heart
or open any door—
and yet hyperbole,
by such extravagance,
overstates reality.

My dear, take no offence.
Your smile is simple,
a mere thing itself,
and yet, through all
its transformations,
it holds to a perfection,
defining and informing
all the rest,
the Shape that shines
above the best.

Ameen, Ahmed

—for Ahmed M, regarding Doaa, Gaza

Oh, we both pray and love the selfsame prayer.
May God walk with her, granting her success.
I will not fret myself and care too much
to know if your Allah is my Allah.
I will say we hear the selfsame God,
His laughing and His weeping. This I know,
like brother, father, friend, yet you as more,
that we both love the selfsame pray-er's eyes,
the dancing of her hands, her rhythmic Grace
wherever her feet go. Where will she go?
Her voice that melts our hearts may warm the world.
This deep-heart woman laughs and weeps and heals.
Ameen, ameen, Alhamdulill'Ahmed.

For Huda in Her Blue Hijab

—for Huda, Ein El Hilweh

Come sit with me and watch the birds.
Arm by arm and hip by hip we'll sit
among the Blue Stars of your garden.
Perhaps our hands will meet in air like wings
of a Blue Rock Thrush the while we chat.
Overhead, a flock of birds, turning,
dipping, weaving, disappearing, purl
their script across the same blue haze
mantling a far-off garden of my own.

Gazapore

—by Omnia, Gaza

My beautiful city with skyscrapers,
depot, seaport, airport.
My Gazapore is famous for
its citruses, olives, and *Kunafa*
which I eat every single day
My hunger can't be silenced
without the juice of them
flowing through me.
I'm Gazaporean.

These things run through my veins
instead of my blood!
And Oh! The mountains,
green orchards, and clear sea.
I can travel outside, but I want to stay.
I have so many pictures of cities
I want to visit, but I don't want to leave.
Rome, Barcelona, London, and New York
are all waiting for me to set foot in them.

No! Gazapore is my homeland, my city,
and my refuge. How can I leave?
Do I not have all I need?

My imagination has run wild.
I've forgotten that Gaza is no Singapore,
no city open to the world!
We are trapped on four sides!
I lack everything: work, electricity,
water, security . . . and freedom.
I can't even see past Erez or Rafah gates.
My enemies go wherever they like.

I can't call my country my own,
while my enemies rename every place in it.
Areeha's citruses wait to be peeled and juiced.
Nasra's olives are ripe enough to be picked.
Nablus's *Kunafa* is ready to be tasted.
Al Jaleel Mountains wait for my footsteps.
Haifa's green orchard greets me.
The Dome of the Rock shines in the sun
and is calling for me.
From where am I, in all of this?

Ah! What's gotten into me today?
I shouldn't think that way!
I've no right to raise my voice.
I've no right to defend my country.
I've no right to dream.
Oh, I've no right to live!

I'm Gazaporean.
That is all.

Wallah, One Light Rises Over Gaza

—for Walaa, Gaza

Fajr

Walaa, your sun will hail from the Levant,
laying crimson, lavender, and gold
atop the Great Omari and Saint Porphyrius,
quickening olive leaves along the Gaza Strip
to their obedient turning through the day.
Mash'Allah, one light illuminates this peace.

Zuhr

Walaa, faithful with the sun, you rise and teach
your wanton boys, so quick to smile or weep,
to rage or sleep, and yet so quick to learn.
They bring you apples, dear, and draw your tears,
and still, bright heart, bright mind, you guide them.
Insh'Allah, that selfsame light will teach them peace.

Asr

Walaa, in rain that cools the rooftop afternoons,
may you dance, as droplets cool your sweat and tears,
not sit and draw your knees up to your face and weep.
Pray to know love's lexicon for rascal boys.
Oh, pray to know what love among despairing men is.
Mash'Allah, their hearts will one day dance in peace.

Magrhib

Walaa, see the blood-red sunset in the West,
as shadows spread across the Mediterranean Sea
and Gazan shade grows deep below the minarets.
One lingering light adorns Omari and Porphyrius.
May Allah tend that selfsame fire in your heart
and warm all weary hearts toward peaceful sleep.

Isha

Walaa, slow your hands across the keys, pause,
and let the night air through the window come.
Rest the coming day and rest the day now done
by kneeling, bringing health to heart and bones.
Untroubled sleep will cover all in welcome night.
Alhamdulillah, Walaa. Dream your dream of peace.

Art by Aya Zakout, with permission

Poor Love Ignites

This passion grabs and drags you where she will,
and down, among the broken, weak, and bent,
while strong men place their bets and test their skill.

They heap and hoard their chips into a hill
and boast triumphant from their high contempt,
but mercy goads and grieves you, as she will.

The widow lays her penny in the till
and in her pauper's kingdom rests content,
while rich men, wagering wildly, flaunt their skill.

To mask cold hearts, they play good fortune's shill.
Their claims, like smoke, conceal the fire they've spent.
Poor love ignites and drives you when she will,

but proffers this one promise to fulfill:
her zeal in burning hearts does not relent,
while made men venture risk beyond their skill.

Though states appraise their hand by strength to kill,
and ploughs reshaped in fear give their consent,
compassion sows and reaps you how she will,
while dead men deal, who staked their lives on skill.

A Psalm for Refugees

—for Dalia and Abdu, Syria/Lebanon

Let aliens inherit the earth,
poor, reviled, homeless beings
probing and violating our borders.

Let us hunger and thirst with them
for righteousness, then all will be fed,
for they too are the children of God.

Let aliens, pleading for mercy,
know the full comfort of our justice
as family, that we too may obtain mercy.

Let us live in peace among aliens,
or they, whose suffering God has seen,
will inherit the kingdom of heaven without us.

A Bird in Qatar

—for Doaa, Doha/Gaza

(*italics, by Rumi*)

Sand, you say, and all the color of sand.
At night, Doha's lights reflect in festive colors
across the bay, where teak and linen sambuks,
ghandajes, and booms rest at anchor,
their high prows reaching moonward.

> *My soul is from elsewhere, I'm sure of that,*
> *and I intend to end up there.*

The streets of Doha are no place to walk,
you say, choked with cars, trucks, and taxis.
It is pleasant in winter, early spring, late fall,
where a blue-green sea laps the beige sand,
and the dhows glide out, their sails full.

> *My soul is from elsewhere, I'm sure of that,*
> *and I intend to end up there.*

You would not trade your life in troubled Gaza
for this; you should not come, you say, to Qatar.
You know I would endure the searing sands,
but Istanbul or Amman, little bird, will be better.
But, oh, Gaza, that sorrowing place, will be best.

> *My soul is from elsewhere, I'm sure of that,*
> *and I intend to end up there.*

In the shade of my maple, while a finch sings,
I imagine you sitting alone far out among dunes
and stones the color of dunes. An old fort,
a child's pale thumb, measures the horizon.
I will find you there, wherever, my friend.

A Voyage of Mo Arafat

—for Mohammed A, Gaza

Pack lightly when you go,
a knapsack, a small case or two.
Your hope will nourish you
from the Negev to the Atacama,
and on to a dead desert
where hot wind sears the soul.

Pack lightly when you go,
a knapsack, a small case or two.
Your voice will carry you
in search of ears that hear,
from Khan Younis to Santiago,
and to the city of deaf men shouting.

Pack lightly when you go,
a knapsack, a small case or two,
as you will haul a great burden,
heavy and awkwardly slung
across your aching shoulders,
like a whole library of books.

Pack lightly when you go,
a knapsack, a small case or two.
Hot winds may wither your hope.
A parched throat may crack your voice.
Your stories may crush you down
and drive your knees into the sand.

Pack lightly when you go,
a knapsack, a small case or two.
Carry your miracle of words
that slake your thirst and feed you,
even as you bend, kneeling there
among the howling winds of D.C.

Moon Over Athens, Ohio

—for Summer and Mahmod, Ohio/Gaza

What will the rising sun bring—

—tree lined streets, cars passing,
children crying in the back seat,
term papers, laundry, groceries,
days filled with friendly voices
mouthing words that never quite
articulate and bring small comfort?

—a wide desert in a troubled sleep,
alone with her small children,
moving and moving toward a horizon,
never seeming closer, no landmark,
wondering how and at what point
she had taken a wrong turn in the sand?

—remembrance of Palestine,
a husband and frail girl in Gaza
whom she carries in her heart,
as she waits for them to join her
far from the country, the water well,
the Friday market with kunafa, dates,
and olives that still feed her soul?

She is tired in her bones.
Her children dream at peace.
When the moon rises among stars
flickering over Athens, Ohio,
she will reach again for her phone.
"Sabah al kheer, Mahmod.
Talk to me, habibi. Make me laugh."

Spin Together

—for Huda, Ein El Hilweh

To lock arms
clap hands
twirl a partner
spin together
through the darkness
of your unknowing
laugh within the rain
of your tears
sing praise high above
the low moans
of your weeping . . .
to love this way
to place your fast feet down
upon the bright ground
of the land
you cannot see . . .
This is your dance
oh dear
my dear
joy in a hope
beyond your horizon

Oh Mothers

—for Rana, Haneen S, Dalia, Duaa, Nedaa, Summer

These are things that I imagine, mothers,
my dear mothers in Gaza, Sidon, Ohio, and Berih:

The rains have passed, the overcast has broken,
the midday blue and billowing clouds gleam
like dreams upon still water resting in a crater.
Rana, see there the faces of your children,
Beautiful and bright, reflecting beside you.

Your hands, Dalia, spread the soil of Berih.
Your grape leaves turn as if in homage to the sun.
A boy stands next to you, watches your hands,
recalling with you another garden with jasmine,
knowing as you know how fragile all things are.

A small boy and a small girl laugh and dance,
while you, Haneen, swirl and sing, your hair flying.
The girl wraps your hijab round her face,
dreams of growing up like you, singing like you.
You yearn for her freedom beyond these walls.

Before sunrise, Duaa, you rise from bed,
your children and your husband sleeping.
You pray, you read, you dance, you wonder when
the gates of Palestine, the world, will open
for your children, their children, their dreams.

Again the rockets startle you awake.
Your children's voices rise with yours, Nedaa.
At your window, both children in your arms,
you watch the stars above a darkened Gaza
on this night, hauntingly clear, and listen.

Late at night, Samar, you hear his voice,
a dream, and while your infant boy still sleeps,
your little girl crawls into bed with you,
and there you talk into the wee hours.
She will see him soon, Insha'Allah.

These are visions you have birthed in me,
oh mothers, dear mothers of my heart.

After a Message from Tarneem

—for Tarneem, Gaza

You walk the beach and stop, like anyone,
to gather shells, let coral sand spill
between your fingers, listen to the sea
repeat its ancient harmony of faith and blood
upon the fabled shore of Palestine.

You could walk the length of Gaza's beach
within a day or two, Tarneem, like anyone,
but there would be an end of it, a threat,
a drone, a fence, a tower with a guard,
a gunboat prowling several miles out.

You messaged me. I love the sea, you said,
then turned until the sunlight caught your face
and made your cheekbone flame against the sky.
Your eyes looked deeper than the sea, my dear,
for all your eyes have seen and heart has dreamed.
Like anyone, Tarneem, you dream, like anyone.

This Would Be Enough

—for Duaa, Sidon

On your balcony,
an hour before dawn,
with our cappuccino,
biscotti, perhaps cheese—
I imagine a juniper nearby.
The chittering finches
and trilling canaries
do not disturb our musing.
To the western horizon,
the Bahr-Motaweset
spreads in pregnant silence
under the warming sky.
This would be enough
to remember you by,
in silhouette raising
a cup to your lips,
your slow, soft sipping,
before saying goodbye,
dear friend, salam.

Holy Dancer

—for Hanin, Gaza

When the mind sings, the heart dances.
When the heart sings, the mind dances.
When Allah knows the music and the dancing
As His own, can you hear His Holy laughter,
Dear Hanin? Can you hear it shake the world?

I have sung with you and danced with you,
And we have laughed together, you young
And I old, you East and I West, yet never met.
Insh'Allah, Hanin, we will share some day
A plate of cookies and a cup of green tea.

Oh, keep singing, dancing, praying thus,
While crying or while laughing, dear Hanin.
Never let your lightsome laughter die, despite
Your sad heavy longing there in Holy Palestine.
Shake the world, Hanin, go shake the world.

Retrouvaille, Ein El Hilweh

—for Pam, Washington D. C.

"A perfect love casts out all fear."

At the Gates of Ein El Hilweh

She wanted in. That is all. Just in. To see a friend.
The burly uniforms bearing rifles scoffed.
What she wanted she would have. That is all.
They saw, correctly had they known, a Tinker Bell.
So she sat down, all childlike and petulant,
with downright Amazonian intent, mid-street,
just waiting for some evidence of manhood
to fill those empty uniforms. And let her in.

They let her in.

II.   Retrouvaille in Al Hamra

We walked along the streets of Hamra,
Looking. Turning. She began to worry,
yet not. She would find them. That is all.
For this I walked the boiling streets of Hamra
(while dodging motorbikes and taxicabs),
this love of hers, downright beatific.
We found the open hearts she knew so well,
waiting in a classroom, hoping. And again,

they let her in.

Allah Here and Now

—for Haneen S, Gaza

Just who does Allah think he is
to test the limits of his patience
by the measure of our failing hearts

Just who does Allah think we are
to test the limits of our patience
by the measure of his inscrutable will

Is it not enough damn it not enough
to see we stumble in the dark
and suffer in the light of day

You let it be enough Allah enough
if we prostrate ourselves and beg
for mercy help relief deliverance

But Allah God! you give us mercy
then ask us still to weep with joy
while children cry—and die—around us

This is personal Allah here and now
I want to sit beside my friend
and hold her while we cry
                              and curse

the evils that yet hold us here
while we stumble in the dark
and suffer in the light of day

Come to us just as you promise
just as you promise come to us
We wait beyond what we alone can bear

Dunya Too Much Defines Us

—for Asrar, Al Salt, Jordan

What became of my wildflower in Jannah?
Spring has come again to the high slopes,
where Allah drapes them all in royal robes.
Neither weed nor gardener troubles them,
yet in a fortnight all their glories disappear.

What became of my wildflower in Jannah?
In the valley, among rubble, along roadsides,
in sunlit vacant lots and sidewalk fissures,
they raise their blue and crimson heads
to greet the passersby, but die ignored.

What became of my wildflower in Jannah?
Elegant hijabs, bright abayas, winsome thobes,
perennial blooms of Allah's cherished garden
fade, and pass, despite our bitter tears.
Dunya too much defines us, dear,

unless our wildflowers in Jannah live
a secret life through all our seasons.
Tell me that our wildflowers grow.
Tell me that our seasons one day end.
Tell me you will be there still, full bloom.

Evening at El Bahhar

—for Doaa and Ahmed M,
Gaza/Doha/Perth

Habibti, the morning qad aata.
Maly araaka still sleeping?
Wake up, it is time for fajr.
Let the adhan tune your heart
To the music of Jannah
And to the sea.

Kif halik? Kif halik, Habibti?
Yalla, lamma ad'ouka, silly!

Now, sleepy head, you rise up
And come to the open window
And look down where I am calling.
Khalas! Yes, be awake now.
Be done with your fajr.
Adhan has finished.

Let me hear your voice calling
"Kif halak, Habibi?"

We'll walk through Souq El Joum'a,
Where the aroma of fresh saj
Seduces us and we'll buy
Enough sabanikh and pizza
For breakfast and lunch.

For supper, we'll sit together
In a corner to ourselves
At El Bahhar and imagine
Sailing in a small ship with white sails
far away, far away, far away.

For the Love of Allah

—for Walaa, Gaza

For the love of Allah, Walaa,
let your soul dance
to tambourine, zill, and oud,
whirl like Sufis, arms flung wide,
and leap the dabka, pound its feet.
By the love of Allah, Walaa,
let your soul dance.

By the love of Allah, Walaa,
let your soul dance,
and do not be afraid.

With breath of Allah, Walaa,
let your heart sing
to drum, qanun, and double flute,
wail and trill with open throat,
and praise with wild, pounding heart.
By the wind of Allah, Walaa,
let your heart sing.

By the love of Allah, Walaa,
let your heart sing
and do not be afraid.

For the love of Allah, Walaa.
By the love of Allah, Walaa.
With breath of Allah, Walaa.
By the wind of Allah, Walaa, fly.

No Wise Word

—for Huda, Ein El Hilweh

You sit on your rooftop
in Ein El Hilweh, facing the sea.

Your heart blazes with a holy fire,
yet finds nothing to consume.

Your hands feel the weight
only of their own emptiness.

Your feet are strong and quick,
yet you have no street to follow.

You read book after book.
Another book is a hamster wheel.

Your words spill into the air
and find no listening ears.

I have no wise word for you,
Huda, that you have not heard.

Allah, why have you put us here?
Allah, why have you put us here?

A Goldfinch lands on your roof,
then continues on its confident way.

Hope

—by Dalia, Syria/Lebanon

Hope visits
on a swallow's wing
to whisper, "I am still here,"
to give lovers
a chance to meet again.

Hope comes seldom
beyond her eyelids,
to promise the little girl
inside of her a sunrise
and a green field
where breezes play
with her long black tresses.

In a Café by the Sea

—for Huda, Ein el Hilweh

Of this essential fire I've seen too little.
It would enflame the whole round Earth
and warm a billion frozen hearts to life,
if frozen hearts were not inclined to flee it.

You, sitting there demure and gentle,
you loved me with that fire in your eyes.
My melted heart poured out in plates
of humus, fries, tabuli, dates, fatouche.

Your quickening fire keeps at bay the ice,
a glacial frost that taunts and tempts my heart
and grips the warmest lands with centuries
of bodies growing cold. Oh Huda, blaze.

Child, I cannot teach you what you know
more truly than I know. Let love compel you
into battle or to peace, as love is heat,
a Holy Scourge that heals what it defeats.

Art by Aya Zakout, with permission

Sniper

—Gaza, March of Return 2018

At 700 meters,
the image remains
picture-like, alien,
with no voice.
A bullet is the fine point
of a rebuttal
to a remote argument.

At 500 meters,
the image gestures wildly
in its silence.
A bullet will erase
the troubling lines of a face,
the widening of its eyes.

At 300 meters,
the image has a faint voice,
but no language.
A bullet will prevent
words forming in the ear.

At 100 meters,
—fire godammit!

the bullet prevents
the odor of sweat,
a recognition of eye color,
the blush in his face
of pride and despair—
and answers smartly
the stone the boy threw.

Ingredients

—for Raneen, Gaza

Insh'Allah, Raneen, we'll share a cake
in Gaza by the sea and trade our recipes.
I'll have a cake prepared for you, you said.

You start by mixing dry ingredients,
the flour, baking powder, and the salt.
You heard the early morning screams, you said.

You then proceed by warming butter soft,
and mixing it with sugar til it fluffs.
You added that a woman lost her son.

You blend vanilla in with eggs, you said,
then divvy in the flour and milk til smoothe.
You said their rockets turned her home to rubble.

When not devouring books at home or school,
you're watching sea waves dance like human beings.
A child died at Erez gate, you said.

You love to write, you said, then sent a poem
on blood-red sunset seas and forgetfulness.
The father cannot stop his surge of tears.

The crème of caramel and cookie crumbs
will glaze the cake, and chocolate flakes will top it.
He fears he'll lose another daughter soon.

You'll bake this shamwah cake for me, you said
with an emoji wink, and send a pic.
And damn this grief, you added last, and stirred.

*Several of the lines borrow terms and images from Raneen's letters to me.

Oh Brother, Great Heart

—for Ahmed N, Gaza

To weep, cry, sob, let fall a deluge—
a heart that holds such passionate skies,
when love bears witness to a suffering soul,
is not small, fearful, weak, and overwhelmed,
but pours its Self like quenching summer rains.

You cradle in your heart, Ahmed, a sea.
Even as you gather up your courage,
steel yourself to circumstance, and fight
through what the treacherous day demands,
Oh brother, great heart, you may freely weep.

So whether righteous indignation,
grief or joy, awe or pity calls,
draw up from your deep reservoir,
the love, alone of all the powers that be,
that hopes and heals and nourishes the soul.
Let fall that rain, Ahmed, across the Gaza Strip.

What Beauty Comes

—for Hanin, Gaza, Spring 2018

Like ambergris or pearl, a treasure forms
when fears and sorrows lacerate the gut
and cut the heart that loves, defiantly,
that knows its life depends on making beauty
from those pains that slay it otherwise.
Out near the fence that clenches like a fist
around the Gazan heart, martyrs are born.
Hanin, what anguished beauty comes of this?
You yearn for simple things, a peaceful day,
for children playing undisturbed by news,
a quiet hour and cookies with a friend,
the freedom of a bird to perch and sing
where dreams that tear its heart may carry it.

We Are Alive, but Dead

—for Dalia, Syria/Lebanon

Hope begins as a hand
reaching for something
then for anything
then for nothing at all
until the empty hand
is too heavy for the arm

> *where are my flowers*
> *dangling over the fence*
> *the smell of jasmine*
> *the gate to my garden*

Hope begins as old shoes
flopping as the feet run
becoming bare feet
plodding along a path
and then only stones
and briars or mud
until fog buries everything

> *I am turning round*
> *and round returning*
> *to the same point*

Hope begins as a heart outrunning
the smell of artillery shells
hearing its own rhythm
as if in a dream
of emptiness and dark
waiting for an impossible song

I am asking and answering
my Self I don't know where I am
this sky is not my sky
these are not my people

Hope ends as a hand
fixing a bowl of soup
combing a child's hair
stroking a man's wet cheek
placing a bouquet of flowers
on a stranger's window sill
and remembering the rhythm
of a song from childhood

*Italics come from a letter written to me by Dalia.

How Many Mornings

—for Duaa, Sidon

How many mornings will pass,
with tea, steam vanishing
against the red and orange
of sunrise over the sea—
How many sunsets will spread
their fiery palettes
across wave and mountain,
delivering their omens—
How many bird songs,
breakfasts, kisses before work,
longings, hopes drawn out
through how many sunsets
casting their dying light
and shadows over dreams—
mists on rivers in Palestine—
that neither live, nor die,
before you can go home?

To A Princess of the Lion Hearts

—for Hanin, Gaza

Keen seer, gallant Gazan,
how you do teach, fierce-fight
and find each logic-lapse,
reason-rive, then shrive by love,
lessoning by laughter, lionness,
princess of the lion hearts.

Tell me what I hear of war
is false, and say the loss I fear,
Hanin, is far. And if that nightfall,
dear, should come, tell me all,
how you will fight, not die,
oh God, that you will call.

It Happens That

—by Hanin, dedicated to Ahmed Abu Armana

It happens that
the loss of one single person
convulses your universe.
You turn numb, robotic, cold.
Then losses fall like hailstones,
until you lose your Self.

It happens that
you keep remembering,
longing, remembering, longing,
longing until your mind empties,
your heart bleeds out,
your soul vanishes.
You are done being human.

It happens that
as a stone splits and gushes water,
your heart shatters and pours out,
you curse love, blaspheme passion,
spit out the last joy of life,
and wish to die.

It happened that
as fighters, steady in their striving,
tunnelled beneath our Gaza,
missiles like vampires devoured them.
Aroma of ambergris rose up from some,
while darkness buried others,
without warning, without ceremony.

It happened
on that blood-red sunset,
as one martyr rose
into the arms of heaven,
his son bloomed on earth.
His widow ululated
as her sweetheart danced in heaven.

It happened, happens, and will happen,
yet we will all gather with them
at the first sunrise of paradise.
A man is never lost as long as
his name and deeds are alive.
He is cradled in the land he dies for.

Soul Running

—for Batoul, Rayan, Dana, Yasmina, Nabil
and Team Walid

Beirut street
summit trail
cool morning
hot afternoon
a marathon
a method
your footfall
following in
your father's

neither to
nor away
from anything
farther out
further in
breath out
breath in
a rhythmic
soul solace

so quietly
you chase
his dream
your own
of running
and resting
south past
the border
of Lebanon

Townsend's Solitaire

—for Doaa, Gaza

Deep among the Highland peaks,
branches toss and sway in the breeze.
Light and shadow move in patterns,
skitter across the forest floor like leaves.
—remembered movements, beloved friend.

A mountain bird, a Solitaire, repeats
its single note; another answers.
And Ravens, jetting overhead,
chatter and chuckle to each other.
—remembered conversations, dear sister.

Far above, a river knows its birth
where melting snows converge.
Here it thunders down in cataracts,
spreads, calms, narrows again and roars.
Will that troubled flow buoy hope, my dear?

Insh'Allah, streams that once converged
will join again, their waters merge and play.
Mash'Allah that feathered voices call,
so let the Ravens haw and hail each other.
Let forest Solitaires call "eep," little sister, "eep."

A Cat in Gaza

—for Raneen, Gaza

A cat, hungry, alert, moves quietly,
hugging closely the walls and fences,
crossing the dark streets timidly,
in search of a suitable home or meal.

Where are your houses, Palestine,
your streets with your ancient names?

Raneen, your heart awakens to Adhan.
A new sun illumines the horizons,
East to West, minaret domes to street,
as you travel home from university.

Where are your houses, Palestine,
your streets with your ancient names?

Among taxis, scooters, and trucks,
past markets humming with voices
of sellers, buyers, children pleading,
you and a cat seek your futures.

Where are your houses, Palestine,
your streets with your ancient names?

Where will the cat nurse her young,
purring, calmly scanning the horizon?
Raneen, at home you dream of Palestine,
of your home becoming home,

of coming and going on ancient streets
more naturally than a contented house cat.

Trees Grow in Jannah

—for Hanin, Gaza

When roots of your heart suck
more deeply from the soil of home
than do the roots of trees,
you do not fear the weather.

A tree dies, but from its growth
comes shelter, heat, and life.

The tree in your memory,
of your dreams,
stands perfectly forever.
Be the child resting
high among its branches.
Be the lover kissing
your beloved in its shade.

Grief for your lost beloved rages
like fire through a forest.
You know that trees grow in Jannah.
There will be no fire.
There will be shade.
There will be the Beloved.

Voices

—by Ghada, Gaza/Doha

On Gaza beach, a girl stops playing.
A storm swirls in her eyes.
She begins whispering a tale,
as if to the waves:

> My land, my home is snatched
> and my dad killed.
> I called out to my mum,
> begging her to bring him back,
> but she too is dead.

Soft and warm is the voice of Jerusalem,
with a deep sigh like a grandmother's
answering with comfort and assurance:

> My old tale was dark.
> My new story will shine.

Voices of Palestinians at home, at work,
echo back as wind stirs,
as if the land itself whispers their hope:

> Our souls are over the moon
> about you, Jerusalem, our city.
> We will smell the soil again.
> We will hold our past in our hands.

We sacrifice for Holy Jerusalem.
We will keep our promise
to set her free.

A young woman,
resting again on Gaza beach,
imagines herself walking,
singing through streets of the Old City:

O, Jerusalem, O, my homeland!
You had my word and you are free.
I died when my family died,
but my heart beats again.
Let's dance with happiness!
Let our voices echo of ages past
and ages to come, O, Jerusalem!
Let's sing all over the world!
Let's cheer around the globe,
Jerusalem is free, she is free.

Such Laughter as She Has

—for Omnia, Gaza, May 2018

Such laughter as she has may echo,
thunder rolling down the distant hills,
booming across a wide valley
of sun shafts on motley fields.

Such laughter as she has will nurture,
spring showers caressing a plain,
whispering through orchards,
rustling through the olive leaves.

Her laughter has room within,
deep enough, high and wide enough
that only dreams can take its measure—

Near the border fence, families gather.

    Tear gas stings the eyes of children.
    Bullets tear the bodies of young men.

Her windows rattle,
    as somewhere in Gaza City,
        a building bursts apart—

In her kitchen, while her mother rests
at the table, one hand at her heart,
she rolls kibbeh, bakes musakhan
and pita for the hummus and oil.

She lifts an arm to dry her cheeks.
She threatens to throw a kubbi ball
at her sister who peeks in the door.

After supper, she will write a story.

She wishes to change the world,
that much, just that much,
she laughs, finger and thumb touching,
as if adding a carefully measured
pinch of salt for perfection of a meal.

Ahmed, Cry Rain

—for Ahmed N, Gaza

Rains bring no justice,
although they yield flowers.

Rains serve no justice,
when they flood wicked towns.

Bullets serve no justice,
even when villains fall.

Bullets bring no justice,
although they yield martyrs.

What use is rain
after the crops have died?

Inheritance

—for Hanin, Gaza

There is a hope that lasts for a day,
until the desert wind blows hard,
pulling the stakes, and the tent falls.
There is a hope that lasts for a year,
until the second winter comes
and the caravan again has no heat.
There is a hope that lasts a half life,
until childhood dreams evaporate,
fortress by fortress, grove by grove.
There is a hope that lasts a lifetime,
until a father dies, a mother mourns,
and the children grow bitter.
There is a hope that endures
and a clinging bitterness with it,
down through all the generations.
Houses are built and fall to decay.
New houses are built and fall to decay.
New houses are built and fall to decay.
Children play in the streets, laughing,
turning their hoops and jumping rope
where children played for generations.
Their inheritance is a bitter hope that lasts,
and among your high and concrete walls,
Hanin, you laugh with them as they pass.

Soar Like a Winged Mare

—for HeBa R, Gaza

Every morning early, I stand inside my bedroom window
and view the mountains, making sure they have not gone.
The mountains are gift. Oh HeBa, how far are your mountains?

I open my gate to watch the clouds and my neighbor's horses.
Before the coming storm, they chase each other across a pasture.
Oh HeBa, you ride swift Nayrooz! Can you ride to your mountains?

In the late evening, in cool air, I lie on my back in the grass
and stare up through the leaves and branches of our maple tree.
The tree is gift, but HeBa, are there olive trees enough in Palestine?

Resting in the finery of my lawn, how shall I think of you, HeBa,
there in Gaza, a stripped and dyng home where hearts lie broken?
I turn and bury my face in the grass, in the shade of my tree.

How do I pray, HeBa, when you fly to forget on the back of Nayrooz,
that hope will fly into your heart and soar like a winged mare?
How shall I pray for you, HeBa, when hope is a gift that torments?

They Say

—for Mohammed A, Gaza

No, Mohammed, our nightly anchors
cannot say military occupation or zionist,
but speak with manicured vagaries.

They will not say that snipers killed
300 protesters this past year,
maimed 1000, wounded 10,000 more.

No, they will not mention children
arrested in Jerusalem, beaten, molested,
detained for days without parents.

No, I have never heard them tell
the stories behind the knives in Hebron,
or the why of rockets hurled from Gaza.

No, they do not explain, not that, and no,
not that either, nor even that. Blah blah,
they say, and sigh, and shake their heads.

Their stories float, as if on air, clouds
of smoke in the shapes of things we think
we already know without asking.

We see smoke, Mohammed,
so we assume a fire, a conflagration,
but we do not see the arsonist.

Instead, we recall a keffiyeh, angry eyes,
a raised Kalashnikov, and we say
we help at least contain that fire.

Insha'Allah, a favorable wind will carry
your poems far, but truth, you know,
flies almost always against the wind.

Art by Aya Zakout, with permission

Carnage at the Said Al-Mishal

—Gaza, Aug. 8, 2018

Hamas had a stockpile there, perhaps,
or three Hamas leaders shared a table and tea
at the Said Al-Mishal Institute for Culture and the Arts.
The library, the theater, the Egyptian-Gazan wives
who gathered there to share their recipes for coping—
all made of paper mache, apparently, mere decoys.
In the office, a secretary, slow to hear the phone,
took a message.

> *Greetings from your Israeli neighbor:*
> *You are advised to clear the building.*
> *You have three minutes.*
> *Alhamdulillah, friend, and salaam.*

And then the stately edifice with cream façade
and brown, mansard roof burst apart,
the Said Al-Mishal Institute of Culture and the Arts.
Amidst the jettisons of block and chair
and window glass from a score of homes,
discordant cries of children, shouts of men,
car horns, sirens confirm that the message
was received.

> *The cultural building our jets destroyed*
> *was a military post, a dire threat.*
> *The people in it were not real.*
> *The culture was not real (8/2018)*

Why the dozen rockets? Did they calculate
the odds of more lost families and little girls,
their fathers and their pregnant mothers?
Yes, indeed, they fear your rockets,
mortars, rifles, kites, slingshots, stones.
They fear far more your grieving eyes
and even more the Said Al-Mishal Institute
of Culture and the Arts.

Are You There, Hassan?

—for Hassan, Gaza

I stir in bed beside my wife,
her warm hip nestled at my side,
the fan's slow whisper overhead.
Flowerets of our blanket match
almost the painting on our wall.

Hassan, you messaged me.
Bully bombs are blowing up
your morning at the school, you said.
Vibrations give disturbing life
to windows, tables, walls, and floor.

Hassan, I tried to reach you, my words
as thin as breath, my fragile beams,
my delicate cables, my only bridge.
Will I betray you if I sleep, if I
awaken to your sentence fragment?

Rana to Sameh

—for Rana and Sameh, Gaza

When the fist of our enemy
closed around the throat
of Gaza and our three children
were hardly more than infants
I held them closely at my chest
and said to you I must be
strong like steel and concrete
cold like ice hot like fire.
They must hear my voice
above the hum of drones
my steady gentle voice
through rain of missiles
my quiet even voice
though full of ice and fire
concrete and steel
yet full of love's laughter
so that we together dear
may cry ourselves to sleep
but not to death.

Hurricane

—for Doaa, Qatar

The reverent heart,
at peace within herself,
may sit along the seashore,
tracing with a finger
in Gaza's coral sand
her longing,
her anguished sobbing,
her deep rage.

Behind her,
remembered and felt,
lies the rubble
of two million hearts
broken,
but still standing,
waiting for a voice
to give them voice.

The reverent heart
may yet articulate
her sobbing and her rage,
sing her longing
for broken hearts,
write, speak,
raise a joyful fist
and fight,
while yet at peace
within herself.

You Dance Your Prayer

—for Haneen S, Gaza

You dance your prayer.
You have no words
but fire,
yet while a sullen, sultry Gaza
sleeps and dreams,
your fire swirls and rises,
burns with fear, sorrow,
an aching of the heart,
and wild joy.
You dance your prayer,
Haneen, in longing,
yearning, keening,
an excruciating beauty.
You dance tonight
with fist raised high.
Your prayer
is that raised fist
and fire.

Judgment

—for Tarneem, Gaza

You stand a meter and a half,
slim and sculpted like a vase.
If you passed with lowered gaze,
your coy, ready smile might chaff
a boy who took you for a child.
Yet craven men have hedged you in,
who fear your judgment for their sin.
The fear that tears their hearts is wild.
They fear your bold and steady pace.
They hem you in with razor wire
and hope the seige will halt your fire.
In truth, Tarneem, they fear your face,
as fire that haunts their dreams is in your eyes,
a thunderbolt from Allah's darkening skies.

Batoul Upon the Seas

—for Batoul, Beirut

As strangers in Al Hamra, we shook hands
across a table, shared polite smiles,
and told our stories, talked of composition.

I taught the power of words to quicken hearts,
to cut or heal, to raise a bitter memory.
You saw the dangers waiting for you there.

Though leagues of ocean lie between us now,
we've gone to sea on words, our fragile skiffs,
as if at first to probe our coastal waters,

then warily to leave the sight of shore
and ply the heavy seas, so broad and deep,
that separate us East from West, Batoul.

Those are mighty oceans that begin as rain
above the hills, then pour as rivers down
through canyon walls and out across the plains.

These are mighty oceans that begin as tears
that wash a billion pair of eyes, or course
like blood in torrents down from broken hearts.

We search among tumultuous waves and swells,
where man-made storms still rage
and gods, as figureheads, are made to fight.

Please tell, Batoul, where calm love reigns,
where we can drift across a placid bay
and grasp our hands in friendship without fear.

May Allah keep you buoyed up, Batoul.
May He, oh God protect us both, my friend,
wallah, I fear the loss of you at sea.

We will shake hands again one day, my dear,
and place our palms against our breasts and touch
our hearts, Christian mine and Muslim yours.

As strangers in Al Hamra, we shook hands.
For now, Batoul, my friend upon the seas
that roar and churn with rage, you hold my heart.

What Binds You

—for Ahmed M, Gaza

What binds you Ahmed, warrior, lover, sage,
as if you dare not speak your mind, unleash
your heart, and free your shackled Gazan soul?

>   *Each morning at your desk, you sift and cull*
>   *and sort impassioned words of editorials,*
>   *and by translation lift their voices, not your own.*

At Rafah gate, the puppets turn you back.
At Erez gate, the puppets turn you back,
while puppet masters manage Ramallah.

>   *Each morning at your desk, you sift and cull*
>   *and sort impassioned words of editorials,*
>   *and by translation lift their voices, not your own.*

Across the fields and fence, small puppets crouch
behind their berms to hem you in with fear.
They pop their guns to keep your fire at bay.

>   *Each morning at your desk, you sift and cull*
>   *and sort impassioned words of editorials,*
>   *and by translation lift their voices, not your own.*

No morning sun has ever risen on its own.
No fiery dawn will rise in you, Ahmed,
unless you put your shoulder to a sun

that lingers til the hour you designate.
Mash'Allah, isnh'Allah, you plead,
as if Allah Himself did not await your voice!

I Too Am Palestine

—for a Palestinian friend, Beirut

A shadow comes and does not rest at first,
but comes again to linger in the wings,
then make a mournful entrance on her stage.

How does this insubstantial thing, mere shade,
impose such weight, as if a heavy sea
were rolling high upon her heart's low shore?

How does this one dark player's aspect
overcast the sky within her heart,
as if a scrim had lowered on her world?

The writers of her stage play left her out,
gave her no voice, no heart, no face, a role
as philistine without a time or place.

Her brief lament, "I too am Palestine,"
a thing to shout with joy, merely dies,
a whisper in the dark that no one hears.

Jeje on the Beach of Gaza

—for Wajiha, Gaza

Israel fears me
because I am.
The world fears me
because I am woman.

You fear my lithe body.
You fear my limber mind.
You fear my fierce heart.
You fear the fire in my eyes.

Let me walk the beach as myself,
without the burden of your fear.
Dare to say you let me.
Just watch me

wear only seaweed,
hang gull feathers in my hair,
crown myself with shells,
hold a driftwood sceptre,

hold a conch to my mouth
and talk back to the sea,
deep speaking to deep,
power singing to power.

Now watch me take my act
down your high halls,
into your pillared chambers
to the head of your table.

Just you watch me

kick sand seaward,
kick sand shoreward,
kick sand in your face,
oh my ruler, my love.

While We Sleep

—for Leen, Gaza

In Palestine, a heavy fog of stereotype
settles over the rubble of 10,000 homes,
of cafes, hospitals, schools, and mosques.

In Palestine, they suffer death
by a thousand foreign cliches,
platitudes, epithets, and dictums.

In Palestine, caricatures drawn abroad
drag behind them shadows falling
in the shape of human beings.

In Palestine, trees fall by the thousands
to an ill wind, but who hears the cries
of those who hear the trees falling?

In Palestine, while we sleep and winds blow,
faint voices send their hopeful texts,
"Knock knock! Are you awake?"

*"Knock knock! Are you awake?" a line of text from Leen to me.

She Dances, She Sings

—for Haneen S, Gaza

She dances,
when he cannot see her.
She sings,
when he cannot hear her.
She weeps,
but he does not hear her.

She rages.
His heart, numb with jobless days,
heavier than a hot night, is silent.

She dreams
that Allah will see her dancing.
She dreams
that Allah will hear her singing.
She prays
that Allah will feel her weeping.

She rages.
Where is Allah when the thunder
of artillery awakens her children?

She dances,
while she sweeps her floors.
She sings,
while her children toss pillows.
She weeps,
when they will not hear.

At Al Aqsa

—by Basman, Gaza

I am praying at his barrier.
He keeps staring at me,
holding his gun and his breath.

Does he feel guilty?
Does he see me?

Can he hear my "Allahu Akbar"
with that helmet on his head?

I kneel on my grandparents' land.
He keeps his "ready to kill" stance.

He tries not to look me in my eye.
I try to hold my tears.

I don't know how I feel.
Should I be angry or scared?

I pray at his barrier.
He points his gun
and holds his breath.

Rana, Imra'a, Spring 2018

—for Rana, Gaza

Rana, search the wardrobe
of your heart for words that suit you.
With what will you define yourself?
Consider an embroidered thobe
from your ancient inheritance,
or an azure, flowing abaya
for an evening in the city,
or the checkered keffiyeh
of a determined warrior.

Home again from a Friday March,
you sit with your children, Rana,
rinsing tear gas again from your eyes,
from their eyes, recalling with them
your fear, your pride, your hope.
You teach them how a beautiful life,
in all of its suffering, its yearning,
and its loving plays out in increments,
like tatriz, one darzah at a time.

Their eyes flicker at your deep gaze.
It is for their quavering hearts
that you stitch their days together
with the words of your stories,
your instructon, and your prayers.
Someday, not far beyond these days
of their youthful impatience, imra'a,
they will search their wardrobes
for patterns of hope you stitched for them.

Physiotherapist

—for Basman, Gaza

If I run from them,
they will not see me breathing.
If I yell at them,
they will not hear me breathing.
If I throw rocks at them,
they will try to stop my breathing.

They pretend I don't exist, or they say,
"You, fanatic! You, standing there
by the Ministry of Health! You, terrorist!
Who do you think you are, Arab,
just standing there and breathing?
Why don't you do something worthwile?"

They speed by, fearful of dying,
grasping their aching chests,
clutching at their angry hearts,
tearing at their hair and gasping
for air after shouting at me.

Through the din of their helicopters
and jets and tank engines revving,
I wonder if any of them says to himself,
"See that man just breathing over there?
I think he is the only one here
who knows what he is doing."

I am trying to teach them how to breathe
by breathing. How else does one
teach the world to breathe?

Dream of Nayrooz

—for HeBa R, Gaza

What are the bursts of light across the city,
the low and jarring rumbles afterward,
as Gaza catches breath.

In a wide pasture,
Nayrooz, with eyes wide, bolts and rears,
pummeling the air, bucking and leaping,
then races ahead of the incoming wind.

Her mane and tail fly, her coat gleams
in the evening light, she and her shadow
as one thing—the mystery of a soul
stirred to exuberant life into a wild joy.

Art by Aya Zakout, with permission

Zombic Irony

Love's agonizing poison eats away
the grandest empires of the world.
A ricin dose will topple fortresses.
This rare, unstable brew, this elixir
of mind, heart, gut, and hand corrodes
and gnaws until the solid, brittle, cold
stone hearts of this undead world
are broken, crushed, warmed
    and healed.

Persistence

—for Ronnie, Majed, Stavit
(the Humboldt Three)

you hear a small voice whispering
a persistent sibilance at first
you know the sound
the smell of it
at that season when
among leaves
breezes prophesy
and probe
the chimney flues
and chinked caulk
of windows
and doors
saying listen
listen

the breezes grow quiet
then speak again and again
until suddenly
the warm
air
bursts apart   in great fists
the whole landscape erupting
a necessary violence of spring
in continuous downpour until
the warmed earth softens and

new   life   speaks
through fissures in the hardened soil

Reaching

—for Hassan, Gaza

among date palms lemon trees
new fig and olive saplings
his hand lifts
to pluck
clean away webs
feel the smoothness
of unripe fruit
as if to test
the firmness of his heart

in motley sunlight and shade
students sit quietly in rows
his hand arcs
to open
cradle a concept
offer up his lesson
for questioning
as if to yield
in sacrifice his own mind

on his rooftop below stars
among water tanks
his fist draws
to strike
an imagined enemy
he turns suddenly
feints parries thrusts
as if to fight
against his mirrored Self

with a small key from his necklace
he unlocks a drawer
his hand pauses
reaching
again for a picture
for his brother's shoulder
his brother's blood-soaked chest
as if to grasp again
a memory too large for a boy's small hand

Paintbrush

—for Malak, Gaza/Istanbul

You, at work intently,
deceptive in your silence,
what is that in your hand?
Your arm moves in and out,
swings wide, then close again,
and sinks, then rises, waits.
You wield a hammer, Malak,
a scalpel, sword, and hoe.
By your adroit hand,
quick and powerful—
oh do not stop to look
and note the slender, soft,
delicate thing it is—
you quicken doleful hearts
or strike hearts down
from Istanbul to London,
New York, Rome, and Paris,
and, oh, mighty Malak,
how you lift your Gaza.
Tease and blend your colors,
human colors, every one,
of blood, skin, bone,
and soul.

On Your Way Home

—for Asrar, Al Salt, Jordan

You on the bus for work,
awakening, rubbing your eyes,
the morning sun gilding
the beige facades of storefronts,
the Great Mosque of Al Salt dome
rising blue against the bluing sky,
random flocks of pigeons
lifting and settling, repeated bursts—
children's laughter.

You on the bus home,
the Al Salt station fading behind,
wheels humming on Q. Rania Street
around and down the hill again,
your mind drifting lazily
to Hammam Street Market,
red, blue, yellow abayas
blending with the scent of breads,
mingled voices rising and falling—
a child's kaleidoscope.

You on the bus again,
to work, to home, to work,
carrying your diurnal hope,
blurred cars and faces passing
days passing along Sport City Street,

sudenly, for an instant,
a reflection, your own face,
your hijab, your own eyes—
a dream of yourself, a prayer

Alchemy

—for Raed, Gaza

Bitter fruit, and sour, sweet Raed,
rolls across your tongue, and yet
the pinch of it does not, too much,
contort your smile into a frown.

You have f-bombed all the world,
Palestine, Gaza, your own street,
swallowed Israel's broken glass,
and yet your heart bleeds joy.

And even so, your laughter spills
from your lips, drips from your chin,
an alchemy of heart-blood made
into the nectar of pomegranate.

A Prayer, to Be Sung

—for Doaa, Gaza

Rest your heart in Palestine,
but little sister, come my way.

From Palestine, little sister,
come away and raise your voice.

Little sister, come away.
Learn your voice in many echoes.

Come away and hear your voice
by many echoes span the Earth.

Send your voice and hear it echo
round the Earth and then return.

Hear your echo round the Earth
and so return a deeper song.

Let it span the Earth and then return
a freer song where your heart rests.

You'll sing your heart for Palestine,
a freer song, insh'Allah,

insh'Allah.

What You Hold In Your Hand

—for Abood, Gaza

What do you hold in your hand, Abood?
What is the shape, the weight, the texture
of your hope?

Hold it up to the sunlight, and as you do,
turn it over and over in your hand
and observe it.

Hold it in front of you, at arm's length,
as you would your thumb,
and measure with it.

Size up the rubble of a shelled building.
Measure the fence that imprisons Gaza.
Gauge the hunger of an orphan.

What you hold in your hand is small,
inadequate in itself, but be grateful
for the genius of your hand.

This is how one may serve, Abdullah.
Continue the slow, patient, crafting
of what your heart desires.

In time, beyond the hoping and despairing,
after the starting overs, you will discover
what hope creates.

Masha'Allah, Malak

—for Malak, Gaza

In the village of Bsharri, I sit at the feet
of Khalil's mountain, gazing long at her,
her curves, her fierce and gentle slopes,
the color of her flesh in the sun comforting
my eyes, her Grace clothed in orchards
and vineyards of peach, cherry, and grape.
I sit among roses, alyssum, and poppies,
gathering light with them, while close by,
the remnants of arz lubnaniy still lift
their arms in longing and lament to her.

The day cools, the haze lifts, the lines,
colors, and shadows of her Grace deepen
like the confident strokes of an artist
who knows my longing, my Mother.
I speak to her. She is silent.

Malak, you have seen her, from far off Gaza.
You have heard her voice in the voices
of mothers, their singing and their weeping.
You know her Grace in the shape of their eyes,
their lips, their shoulders, their breasts.
I see in the work of your palette and brushes,
the sternness, the laughter, the sorrows
of her brow, and I say, "Now she speaks to me.
I see your mothers of Gaza, Malak."

Brothers, You Give Me Laughter

—for Basman and Bassem, Gaza

From a high place, even from a minaret,
oh, let me look down into Gaza and see
the full space of her suffering.

From a low place, a hollow in the sand
of her beaches, let me touch (how can I?)
the wide waters of her separation.

From a dark place, even a dank basement,
no, the bottom of a crater, let me smell
the blood-depths of her despair.

Oh! And then, allow me to sit in the sunshine
of a street café and taste the dark
honey of your laughter, my brothers.

A Bird Flees Her Cage

—by Haneen H, Gaza

She drew her legs up to her torso,
folding her arms in an embrace.
Turning to fantasies of romance,
she tried to sleep, but burning stars
beyond her cage held her wistful eyes.
She dreamed of being a goldfinch,
no fragile damsel in a fantasy.
She dreamed beyond horizons.
A horizon never arrives,
never becomes a boundary.
The silver lining is a sun rising,
beyond clouds that never sink.

She could not rest in fantasy,
when the occupied lands, her lands,
lay so close, her sunlight
gleaming from her wheat fields,
glimmering from her olive trees,
flashing against the domes
of her mosques,
where soldiers did not exist.

A whisper interrupted,
"Would the soldiers fire at me
if I crossed the boundary?"
The question robbed her freedom.
That fearful question held her captive.
Her fantasy did not allow her to speak
of the terrible reality in her thoughts.

She could dream whatever she wanted.
She could make boundaries disappear.
She could make giant waves
swallow the occupier's ships.
She could make this all disappear
in the blue dim light of her room—
the borders, the crisis, the soldiers.

Peregrine, the Heart Is Its Own Sky

—for Mohammed M, Gaza

Hail, raven-headed beauty, my Mohammed!
I hear your peregrine voice, heart-raptor,
Keening in heart-hunger for her, your city.

Where is she? You, held captive on a perch,
How will you find her, how soar above her,
Then rest among her domed roofs by the sea?

She lies broken, weeping and waiting for you.
She lies on her side, wounded and sleeping.
She dreams of a warrior with strong wings.

Hail, dark lover, you are not captive beside her!
The heart is its own sky! Open your eyes. See her.
Grasp her shoulder, awaken her, teach her again to fly.

Dreaming in Gaza

—for Leen, Gaza

"I see better now with the eye of wisdom,
not with a wide eye, and yet a light comes through."
                              —Leen, from a letter to me

My hungers grow deeper, desperate.
The knot in my stomach doubles me over,
mostly through the long hours of every night,
until I sleep and dream, then dream again,
until the Adhan draws me up from slumber.

I aim my prayers at Allah. I listen to wind.

I reach my hand into a dusty box,
rummaging for old scraps of wisdom,
notes on Gaza's vendors, relentless cars,
sidewalk cafes, redundant wars, stray dogs,
the smell of fish and sewage on the beach.

I find no plot line, no characters developing.

I dreamed last night of whirling dervishes,
spinning in their passion, skirts billowing,
as placid as a row of flowers without breeze,
content to be in that one place, unmoved,
and yet gone far and further on their journey,

joyful, exuberant, spinning to somewhere.

Where is my motion, my whirling dance
to somewhere certain, away from the Gaza
clenching at my stomach, or through?
If I circle inward far enough, will I burst
upward into joy, toward a fine point of light,

joyful, exuberant, a direction in which to rest?

Dalia, Bright Leaf

—for Dalia, Syria and Lebanon

Such things as these define you,
Dalia, daughter of Allah's spring:

evanescent April snow
bright buds bursting husks
twig tips lifting pushing
new leaves furled unfurling

Through spring and summer,
leaves sway east to west,
diurnal devotees of sun.
Light that empowers them
powers the whole earth,
drives the deep water
that drives their roots.

Garden plot or saladat al-Salat,
such things as these define you,
dear, bright leaf in Allah's light.

A Prayer

—for Asrar, Al Salt, Jordan

May Allah welcome you,
with bright sky and flowers,
their light reflecting back to you
the Graceful beauty he has given you.

May Allah show to you,
with high trees and mountains,
his mighty power within your heart,
much greater than the strength of any arm.

May Allah call on you,
with wind and rushing waters,
and by such soft and fearsome beauty
teach your soul the many powers of your voice.

An Evening Without Horizon

—for Hanin, Gaza

Shahada

From a high window, Hanin, see
the minarets in stately pairs rise
beside the Mediterranean shore,
delicate, steadfast in their reaching.

Salat

They await the adhan, the maghrib
to sing in melancholy, fervent notes
and link the evening blue of Gaza
to the azure and lavender sunset.

Zakat

Who will come to the aid of Gaza,
this broken city, bringing succor,
a heart's kunafa and maftoul enough,
the morning feast from Heaven?

Sawm

Within an hour, a general darkness
will unite the Heavens and the Earth,
stars answering the lights of Eid al Fitr,
when all creation feasts as one.

Hajj

You yearn, Hanin, for an embrace,
a drawing together of mind and heart,
a stranger's face become familiar,
a freedom far off brought home.

Heart Rhythm

—for Duaa, Sidon

In the morning, oh Lord,
you hear the voice
of one crying her dua.
In the morning, oh Lord,
you hear the pad pad
of her feet dancing.
The dance too is her dua.
Your daughter by the sea,
Duaa, calls to her children.
She hears their voices.
She feels the pitter-patter
of their feet on the floor
like her own heart rhythm.
Let the cries of Duaa
be the echo of your voice.
Let the dua of your Duaa,
dancing by the sea,
be like the eternal rhythm
of your own heart, Allah.
Let your laughter be laughter
of her children, be her own.

Biographical Sketches—the Friends I Celebrate Here

Abdullah

("Abood")—My nickname is Abood. I believe that one's identity has many facets. I define myself as a son, a brother, and a 20-year-old English Literature major from Islamic University, Gaza. More fundamentally, I define myself as a Palestinian. I therefore share in one of the world's most threatened identities. As a writer, I hope that my work will someday advance and preserve my at-risk Palestinian culture. My grandmother, Khadra, has taught me more than anyone else about my ethnic and cultural roots. She has shared with me her many sad memories, but has also taught me hope.

—Abood first contacted me, asking for help with his English language skills. Over and again, he impresses me with his deep sense of integrity, his tireless hard work, and his affection for his family. It has been a profound joy to become friends with him and his entire family (mother, father, sister, brother, and grandmother). He plans to come here soon. I want to get the house ready, and a list of things we can do. If the weather is bad (or not), we'll have plenty to talk about.

Ahmed M

I am 25, a graduate of English Literature from Al-Azhar University, Gaza. Currently, I am studying for a master's degree in International Relations at the University of Queensland, Australia. Through conversation and reading widely, I nurture interests in a variety of interests, in global politics, philosophy, world theologies, Arabic poetry, and calligraphy.

—I love Ahmed for his spiritual insights and gentle, compassionate nature, and especially for his courage in facing his fears and finding

*a way out of Gaza, in order to pursue his education and live close
again to a woman he loves. I said to him once, "Ahmed, love IS
courage." Someday, I will sit down with Ahmed, and we will talk
about human nature, politics, and Allah, for hours, for days.*

Ahmed N

I graduated from Al-Azhar University in Gaza City, with a
bachelor's degree in English Literature. Born in the middle
of Gaza, in the community of Deir Albalah, my dream is to
advance the cause of Palestinian human rights and to expose
the "human face" of the Israeli occupation. Now at 24, I am
in my third year as project manager for the Gaza team of We
Are Not Numbers (www.wearenotnumbers.org).

*—Ahmed knows suffering common to most Gazans living under
siege. He has also suffered torture and imprisonment at the hands
of corrupt police outside of Gaza. He has shared his heart with
me, and I do not have words enough to say my admiration for
him. I share with him a wrestling with this question: How do we
love, after suffering? He and I will continue talking about love,
the impossibility of it, the imperative of it, the necessary risks in
it, the joy and healing that comes from it.*

Ali

A writer for We Are Not Numbers, I am an English
Language and Literature graduate from Al Azhar University,
Gaza. My understanding of myself and the world was shaped
significantly by a year studying abroad in Chicago, Illinois,
USA. I think of myself as a dreamer and a tea-and-book
enthusiast, Palestinian by blood, yet American in spirit. I
love drama, music and learning languages. In addition to
English, I know a little French, Turkish, and Hebrew.

*—Ali brings joy, to me and to many. Like so many in Gaza,
nearly all, he struggles with a profound sense of how hope and*

despair exist inextricably together in the heart. I have not yet been to Gaza, but already I feel welcomed by many—Ali embodies that welcoming. His easy, jovial manner does not readily betray his highly capable and deeply serious mind. The nine-hour gap between us is frustrating, as is the fact that Gazans have electricity only a few hours a day. "We gotta video chat soon."

Asrar

My name means "secret." I am passionate about travelling and exploring new places and new people. I love art and history, and I love to visit museums and attend musical theatre. Currently, I am a lawyer and human rights advocate, specializing in migrant workers' rights. I love helping such vulnerable people, despite it being an emotionally exhausting vocation. I aspire to pursue new experiences, especially while learning more about the causes and effects of the migrations of peoples.

—I met Asrar here in the US, but talked with her only briefly. We have stayed in touch online, and our deepening friendship has been a great joy and a multi-faceted blessing, her spirituality, her intellectual questing, her love of travel . . . Asrar explores. Asrar's depth of determination, her ruthless self-honesty, and her high aspirations inspire me as a friend, writer, and fellow traveler. Our road is often the same, I think.

Aya

I'm 19 years old, studying dentistry at Al-Azhar University in Gaza. I hope one day to become a great artist and dentist at the same time and to give solo exhibitions in Gaza and beyond. I currently sell my original artworks to people in several countries. I hope to open my own dentistry clinic here in Gaza, where I can also display my works. Life in Gaza so hard. It is difficult, impossible really, to describe all of the ways that life here tears us down. We survive day by day, trying to do what we love, despite the stress and the frequent traumatic news. I go to school every day, simply wanting to do what I love. I keep a smile on my face.

—*Aya's artwork caught my eye before I knew anything about her. I assumed that someone at least mid-20's had produced such gorgeous mandalas; then I learned that Aya was only 17 then. Her art displays a wonderful creativity and freedom, along with a meticulous attention to detail. The requisite patience seems rare in one so young. Getting to know Aya as a friend these past two years has been a joy and an inspiration, as I witness her beautiful art emerging from a warm and playful heart under profoundly difficult circumstances.*

Basman

I am Basman, single, 30, a physiotherapist, and a writer. I love poetry, music, reading, cooking, basketball, and movies. My greatest hope is to find freedom, both within and beyond Gaza. A bird cannot fly, cannot fully live, inside a cage.

—*I hardly know what to say beyond what my poems tell. Basman calls me brother. I cherish his profound insights and his humor, especially his dark humor born out of the suffering that his own writing chronicles. His name translates loosely as "laughter." I love his choice of political memes (I won't mention any particularly colorful person here). We laugh often. Our chats turn serious often. He is a brother in laughter and tears.*

Bassem

I am Bassem, single, 30, a poet and script writer hoping to be an actor. I am founder of the video-production group, Abnormal Team for Acting and Art in Gaza. Much of my time involves serving as a volunteer for the Fares Alarab Organization, as Youth Program Coordinator.

—*Bassem and Basman are twins (Bassem also means*

"Laughter"). I met Bassem in the US at the same time I met Asrar. Our friendship began here and has endured time and distance. I love his comedic videos, rising as they do from such troubled circumstances. In this brother, I know a great heart and heart-warming smile. I hope one day to sit with Basman and Bassem and listen to them tell me jokes that will make me cry.

Batoul

I am 23 years old and a Business Administration graduate. After college, I got heavily involved in sports, not only to stay physically fit, but also to nurture my mental health. I love table tennis. I have run a number of half-marathons and a marathon. Athletics help relieve my daily stresses and build friendships with many wonderful human beings.

—Batoul attended the writing workshops that Pam and I hosted in Beirut, in the summer of 2017. I remember quickly feeling an easy kinship and affection, and yet a deferential respect for this young woman with a sun-bright smile, a bold presence, and an unwavering sense of dignity. Someday, I will see her run a marathon, immediately after which I might have a slim chance of beating her at table tennis.

Dalia

My husband Abdu and three sons lived in Syria until the civil war began. We fled into Lebanon, where we have lived for nearly seven years. I have worked as a teacher, while Abdu has done construction work. We have no job security, and our status in Lebanon is very fragile. We stand on the strength of our hearts, not of our feet. We measure time by hope, as we wait for divine justice.

—"Tell me what to do, Kevin. What should I do?" Dalia asked these questions of me in Beirut, where she had come to help us in the writing workshops. Dalia teaches me about hope, the twin of despair,

the heaviness and pain of hoping through impossible circumstances. She is a humanitarian, a teacher—and a friend of the kind that makes time and distance feel both painfully frustrating and yet irrelevant. Dalia is a beautiful and generous soul, a joy.

Doaa

I am a 23-year-old free spirit and wild dreamer. I graduated from Islamic University-Gaza, spending one semester of study abroad at Carroll College in Helena, Montana, USA. I recently finished my master's degree in Translation at Hamad Bin Khalifa University in Doha, Qatar and currently work in the Teach for Qatar Program. I hope to earn my PhD, somewhere in the world.

—What can I say beyond what I said in the dedication of this book? Haha, on one hike in the Highland Mountains, Doaa became so enraptured by the beauty of the forest that she left the trail and began running and laughing among the trees . . . or I could tell about her essay, "The Teachings of War," . . . or . . . This young woman changed my life. She holds a deep place in my heart.

Duaa

My favorite nickname is Whisper. I am comfortable alone and tend to be very quiet. I love my home life as wife and mother of two. As an educator and dreamer, I carry a strong faith in the power of children to learn. I believe deeply in their potential to grow up and change our world for the better. I love three things for escaping my stressful world: an early morning, a cup of green tea, and a plant-decorated balcony.

—I knew that I would never forget the people I met and worked with in Beirut, but I assumed that they would not long remember me. After all, "Who am I? Just an aging nobody from Montana," as I have said to them. Duaa remembered me, and while I have not yet met her husband and children, I dream of doing so, as I

feel like a member of the family. She tells me that they ask often about "our American friend." I know in her a deep mutual trust and hold for her a great affection and admiration.

Ghada

I am 28. I studied English at the Islamic University of Gaza and am now pursuing a master's in Audiovisual Translation in Qatar. I am very interested in psychology, as I believe it is important to understand both human behavior and the inner world. Reading is my inspiration and writing is my passion. I come from a land that "has never seen peace," but flowers, birds, rain, music and the beach are my source of peace. What I am crazy about the most is vintage stuff. My dream is to run a flower shop and learn horseback riding.

— *Over the past year and a half or so, I have admired Ghada's patience, her gracefulness, and her insightfulness, as she has carried her hopes past obstacles and setbacks. She finally found a way out of Gaza and into Qatar for graduate school. I learned, finally, or perhaps just temporarily, how to pronounce her name correctly, through her graceful patience and persistence in teaching me.*

Haneen H

I am a Pakistani-born Palestinian. As a third-year college student, I study Physics, but I have many interests. After moving to Gaza, my interest in writing and history deepened. The more I was exposed to the truth, the more I wanted to know, and the more I wanted to write. I have always been fond of astronomy as well. When I am not busy counting the dimensions of our universe, I'll probably be holding rusty tools and fixing broken stuff or solving puzzles with my younger sister.

—*I cannot think of Haneen without smiling, and maybe wincing a bit, given her keen wit and unsparing critiques of my poetry. She loves the straightforward, blunt, and honest—just like her mother, she says. She believes in the power of words, and quotes Malala Yusafzai, "Just one book , one teacher, and one pen can change the world!" So when I think of Haneen, I think "wry, good-natured fire," good for the mind and soul. And just plain fun.*

Haneen S

I studied secretarial skills at Al-Aqsa University in Gaza, but then got married at the age of 19 and soon had two children. Now, at 25, I am a writer working toward becoming a peace researcher. One of my favorite quotes is "to be seen is to be loved."

—Haneen and I have talked about her life in Gaza, crippling poverty, motherhood and marriage, Gazan society, strength and weakness, and God—the Allah who is here and not here, faithful and absent. We have talked about dancing, for joy when joy comes, and defiantly when joy does not. She sings, beautifully. I know of no one who wrestles more deeply and determinedly with self and circumstance.

Hanin

I was born in 1995 in Khan Younis, a city in the Gaza Strip, in occupied Palestine. I graduated from the English Literature department at the Islamic University of Gaza and am finishing my master's Degree in Linguistics. I currently work as a translator and content writer in the Cortoba Technologies Company. I also love poetry.

—Hanin teaches. I send drafts of poems and essays; I send ideas. Her critiques and musings teach me. Four things come together in my understanding of Hanin: a brilliant analytical mind, a deep and resolute faith in Allah, a kind and gentle heart, and beautiful conversation. Will there be time enough for a long walk on the beach? A giant plate of cookies?

Hassan

I am 22 years old and live in Gaza City, Palestine. From my early childhood on, I have struggled to achieve self-confidence and dreamed of seeing my people empowered. I practice martial arts and love to spend time in my family's gardens. While I love studying English Literature and currently enjoy teaching, I aspire to be a successful businessman. Insha'Allah, I will achieve my dreams.

—Hassan has a way of getting an especially important message across to me, again and again: Just keep getting stronger. He teaches, lifts weights, practices martial arts, tends gardens, and vents his frustrations with Gazan government, Israeli oppression, lack of professional opportunity, and frustrated romance—yet I get from him that same encouragement: Just keep getting stronger.

Heba A

I grew up in Gaza, but moved with most of my family to Turkey, so that I could study on scholarship there. I see myself as a loving humanitarian and a Palestinian with a Gazan heart. I am a 19-year-old dental student in Ankara. I am addicted to coffee, novels, and nature.

—Heba works very hard and diligently, and yet I believe that learning comes somewhat easily or naturally to her. She is bright, and very. I suspect that her joy does not come so easily, as it does not for anyone in or from Gaza, and yet the bright energy of her youthful joy is contagious, delightful, and uplifting. Her adult insights are quick and deep.

HeBa R—*

—Heba and I communicated often for about a year and a half, but she suddenly disappeared from Facebook and Instagram and stopped responding to emails. She loves to write, published a

book in Gaza, and finds great joy and a deep sense of freedom in riding horses. Sadly, she had to sell her horse, in order to pay for college. Not long after, she went silent.

Huda

I graduated with a bachelor's degree in Economics from the American University of Beirut. The lack of opportunities here for Palestinian refugees means that many people, including me, struggle to find suitable jobs. Circumstances do not get easier, yet I keep reminding myself of my hopes and dreams and that the things I am passionate about are worth living for, including writing.

—Huda is a quiet fire—a passionate advocate for Palestinian rights, a thinker, and a compassionate soul. As a resident of Ein El Hilweh refugee "camp," Huda understands more keenly than most the discouragements of under-employment and the extreme stresses of sectarian violence. She worries that sharing her griefs and frustrations might burden me, but in fact her sharp wit and deep affection, her lightsomeness, often lift me.

The Humboldt 3

The Humboldt 3 were put on trial in Germany for protesting against an Israeli official, in June of 2017, at Humboldt University in Berlin. The three activists highlighted the Israeli official's responsibility for war crimes and crimes against humanity. Ronnie Barkan says, "The Humboldt trial is a great example of the power of cracking through a discourse of lies. Clearly pointing the finger at the real issues at hand has its consequences, even in being legally and physically attacked by the authorities. These are the telling signs of speaking truth to power, yet are in fact a reason for optimism that real change could be just around the corner."

Majed Abusalama

I am a Palestinian scholar and award winning journalist, having earned the UNESCO/IFEX Freedom of Expression Award 2011 for my courage and activism. I prefer, however, to be called a justice and human rights fighter. I was born in Jabalia refugee camp in Gaza, Palestine, where I co-founded the Intifada Youth Coalition that organized many non-violent demonstrations along the Gaza fence. I am a founding member of several NGOs, initiatives, and campaigns in Gaza. I now live in Berlin, Germany, fighting all forms of discrimination, especially anti-Palestinian repression

Ronnie Barkan

I am an Israeli dissident, a BDS activist and serial disrupter to apartheid representatives. Rather than dealing with the honest right-wing Zionists, I'd rather focus on shedding light on the far more racist and sinister form of Zionism, which comes under the guise of so-called 'liberal Zionism.' It is that discourse which protects and promotes Israeli crimes against humanity in the mainstream media, and whose leading tool of propaganda is Haaretz newspaper.

De. Stavit Sinai

I am a scholar and Israeli-Jewish dissident. I teach philosophy in Berlin and promote civil disobedience, as well as intellectual resistance to apartheid. I am the author of "Sociological Knowledge and Collective Identity" (Routledge 2019), and the recipient of the Junior Scholar Prize (ISA, Japan 2014).

Leen

I am a Palestinian with a B.A. in English-French literature and on my way to earning a master's degree in Italy. I speak five languages: English, French, Italian, Arabic and human. I write in English and Arabic and have contributed stories to We Are Not Numbers. I live with an Israeli drone in my head, day and night, but wherever I go, I pursue peace. I believe in active communication as a major key to success. I am not perfect, yet I seek balance and wisdom. I appreciate something Kevin said to me a while back: "I belong to Allah alone. Sure, you have weaknesses and failures, but knowing WHOSE you are will lead you to know WHO you are."

—*Leen and I have enjoyed poignant conversations about faith, spirituality, and romance. She has at times asked me for advice and perspective, but I remember once telling her this: "You already know the answer. You already have the wisdom you seek." Like so many young Gazans, perhaps all, Leen struggles deeply with the sense of futility and humiliation that a military siege imposes on her. And yet. And yet her compassion, her humility, and her wisdom prove the immeasurable scope of a human heart.*

Malak

I am 19, originally from Gaza, Palestine. I began painting at 13, during the 51-day Israeli military assault on Gaza in 2014. We had to stay indoors for safety, and my painting became a way of releasing my negative energy—fear, anxiety, and sheer terror. For my earliest paintings, I used watercolors and paper from school. Painting has opened up a whole world of self-expression for me, and I have now finished over 300 paintings. I first began showing paintings to a Gazan audience, but also shared my work with an increasing number of friends around the world through social media, especially Facebook and Instagram. My artwork has now been featured in solo and group exhibitions in Jerusalem, France, Spain, Turkey, Costa Rica, India, England, and in 11 states in the USA, including an Art Under Siege exhibit in the Rayburn House Office building, US House of Representatives in Washington D.C.

—In the summer of 2017, I sat near the Khalil Gibran museum, looking southward along the eastern slopes of Mount Lebanon, reflecting upon the common themes of Gibran's paintings. I could not help but think of Malak Mattar's art, her astonishing intellectual depth at 17 years old, and her own quiet, confident, and queenly aspect. As is the case with perhaps all serious artists, Malak weaves together within herself and in her paintings a playfulness and stern seriousness.

Mohammed A

I come from Gaza, Palestine and have travelled extensively through Chile and the northeastern USA. Throughout my travels, I have given presentations about the Palestinian struggle for freedom and dignity. My dream is to see Palestine become an independent nation. I have a bachelor's degree in TESL from Gaza and am completing an internship in Washington D.C. for US Congressman Donald Payne.

—Moe's poetry chronicles what his people experience in Gaza: relentless humiliation and terror under siege, an aching pain of loss, and a longing for a home that they can again call home. Moe has traveled far more now than most Gazans, but at every border, he faces prejudice. Considering his expansive heart and ready smile, his desire to explore and connect, I think the whole of planet Earth is not big enough to contain even one human heart. During his travels here, time, distance, commitments, and finances have prevented us meeting, so far. Ignorant and self-serving politics create the more intractable barriers.

Mohammed M

If I recall correctly, Mohammed is 27. My communication with him ended after about a year. He is an English language instructor and an aspiring poet with great potential.

Nedaa ("Nadoosh")

My name is Nedaa, but family and friends call me Nadoosh. I am 29 years old, married, and mother of two. I studied English Literature, and I now work in Gaza, Palestine for Doctors Without Borders. I love writing and everything that lets me feel human—especially helping people and making them smile.

—Nadoosh has a strong sense of who she is. Like women everywhere, she has had to fight for her identity, but she has help. Her husband stands shoulder to shoulder with her. I have been blessed to learn from her wisdom, her tenacity, and her longsuffering. Our conversations about marriage, childrearing, and the development of an autonomous Self have often challenged me to rethink my own understandings, which often come too easily, given my comparatively easy life circumstances. Nadoosh is a resonant sounding board and a kind friend.

Omnia

I am a 23-year-old writer from the Gaza Strip, Palestine. I have many poems and a collection of short stories published in Arabic. I am also winner of an international short story prize for a story in English. I work as a freelance translator and writer.

—I imagine sitting down with Omnia and both of us bursting out laughing (or crying?) before either of us says a word. I like to think we have an understanding. I am stronger and, I hope, wiser from knowing Omnia. She lost her mother several months ago. I watched her sink into grief and self-doubt and silence, knowing that she would surface again, stronger and wiser. I misread one of her poems recently and got a faithful poke in the ribs—and a good laugh.

Pam

I am a freelance writer and social-justice activist working full-time for an NGO based in Washington, DC. I lived and worked in the Gaza Strip for three years immediately following the 2008/9 Israeli assault. I have traveled extensively in the Middle East, including a journey to Yemen and Pakistan to interview people impacted by imperialist drone surveillance and warfare. My writings can be found on sites such as Truthout, Alternet, Mondoweiss, Middle East Eye and Al Jazeera. In addition to my full-time work, I am also founder and International Director for We Are Not Numbers.

—Through Pam and Doaa's invitation, I began working first as a mentor for We Are Not Numbers (WANN) and then, in the summer of 2017, helped Pam conduct writing workshops in Beirut, for Palestinians in Lebanon. I have written and taught writing for years, but working with Pam pushed me into some new frontiers for learning the transformative power of narrative, of truth-telling in a politically charged and dangerous context.

Raed

I am 22 and live in Khan Younis in the Gaza Strip, Palestine. I study English Language and Literature at Al Azhar University. I love movies, tv series, and wrestling, and I hope to become a screen-writer and perhaps an actor. I also dream of becoming a writer, commentator, or manager in the wrestling world. I guess that seems crazy, but that's something I really want to do. I hope most to write fiction that becomes movies and tv series. I hope to write something as good as Breaking Bad.

—I began communicating with Raed just months ago, connecting with him through mutual friends. I had enjoyed his often sardonic posts for several months before that, noting some things deeper

than his seeming cynicism: his determination to keep laughing, his self-deprecatory humor, and his tenacious hopefulness coupled with a devastating realism. So I said to myself, "This guy is funny, and he spares no one, least of all himself, from his darkly ironic humor. I need to get to know him."

Rana

I am an author, mother of triplets, wife of a good man, proud Palestinian, and lover of all that is human. Oh, and I'm also a Sherlockian.

—Rana said to me recently that nothing fascinates her anymore, and yet a long and deeply engaging conversation flowed immediately from her self-disparaging comment. Rana has participated in the Great Return March several times, perhaps— and here I speculate—as her bodily way of saying, "Enough talk. Now what do we DO?" And there the ever-present siege, the fence, the kill-zone surrounding Gaza, wants abruptly to cut all conversations short. So we talked at length about the definitions of love, the interplay of justice and mercy, and coffee and movies and.

Raneen S

I am 21. I study English Language at the Islamic University, Gaza. I adore poetry, both reading and writing. My favorite poet is Shakespeare. Currently, I work as an assistant teacher for Alsalam Training Group.

—In a poem, Raneen asks, "If that tear on Mohammed's mother's cheek could speak, what would it say? Would it speak the pain of unspoken, unforgettable days?" Most of my conversations with Raneen center on the mundane, her lesson plans for schoolchildren, my writing or hiking, her own schoolwork. I help her interpret a text; she sends steady encouragements from Gaza in return. In her pictures, she smiles. I sense in her, even

in her smiling pictures, a defiant joy and a defiant hope against the odds.

Raneen Z

I'm 22 years old, studying literature at Islamic University, Gaza. I write poems in order to reach beyond my own world. In my poetry, I translate my feelings and describe my experiences, with the hope that my thoughts and feelings will reach readers outside of Gaza. I believe that as I write for others, my words can break the siege and silence imposed upon us.

—I keep insisting that Raneen make a carrot cake for me when I visit Gaza, and then our chats turn to English slang terms, revising one of her poems, her family's new house, our favorite recipes, or staying up late to write. It seems we end up laughing through every chat. We work together in order to improve her English, the reason she contacted me to begin with. Her progress has been remarkable. We do not often discuss the regular Israeli assaults against Gaza, but we grapple with questions of faith, endurance, and hope. She hopes to become a published author. She has much to share with the world.

Salsabeel ("Sal")

In October 2010, I left the country I was born and grew up in, the UAE, and moved with my family to the biggest open-air prison on earth, the Gaza Strip. In August 2019, I finally managed to escape Gaza and return to the UAE, but alone, without my family, whom I probably will never see again. I guess this is a reality that many Palestinians have to live with for the rest of their lives.

—Salsa has quipped about her short, childlike stature (but I think she likes it). I enjoy the irony of that, given that she wields a truly powerful mind. Her posts reveal an astonishing depth

and breadth of reading, of insight into what she reads, and of mental agility. A spirit so strong, adventurous, passionate, and playful as hers needs a wide-open world. Her life in crowded and constrained Gaza forced her to discover and explore her vast inner territories and resources. She lives in Abu Dhabi now, a step closer to freedom.

Summer

I am 34 years old, married, with three lovely angels. I am a lifetime learner who never quits. My passion is giving hope to those who most need it. If I give hope to one person on this earth, I am a winner.

—For nearly two years, I had the privilege of helping Samar as editor, mentor, and friend. She recently finished her master's degree in Ohio, then moved to Canada with her family. I have told her, and yet I doubt she fully comprehends, what a powerful source of encouragement and inspiration she has been to me. And what a joy it has been to witness the thought processes of such a powerful mind. I pray her voice will be heard, widely. And yet, what I most want to say is that Samar is a dear friend.

Tarneem

I am 25. I was born in Saudi Arabia, but now live in Gaza. I graduated with a bachelor's degree in English Literature from Al-Azhar University. For part-time work, I serve as both a teacher and translator. I believe that to teach is to touch a life forever.

—Tarneem has spoken, fearlessly, of her fears—of war breaking out again, of not being able (or perhaps even willing) to live through it again; of the sheer mind-bending, heart-twisting horror of it. I suspect, nonetheless, that her students feel from her eyes and her smile the steady warmth of compassion that I do. She delights in them. I know this, by pictures from her classroom *of her students, their work on whiteboards, their Christmas art, the joy in their eyes and humble pride in her own.*

Wajiha ("Jeje")

I am a Palestinian living in Gaza, but originally from Jaffa. I earned a bachelor's degree in English and French Literature. Currently I work as a producer at Zainab Production Company. I have produced documentaries mainly about the Palestinian cause and culture. My interest in writing started when I was quite young. I later joined We Are Not Numbers, in order to publish my stories. I love to write personal stories, highlighting issues rarely addressed in my society, especially women's lives and rights in the Middle East. I am also part of Political Is Personal, an online platform for Palestinian and Israeli women to share their stories with the world.

—I came to know Wajiha first as "Jeje." She loves the beach, loves to read, and loves to speak truth. She has the writer's "voice" for it. Jeje's writing tends to catch my breath. She often addresses conditions of a besieged city, but with the depth of someone grappling the fundamental questions of what it means to be human. In one poem, she asks, "Am I standing on my feet?" and says, "I collapse with the words I write." Ironic that, as she has been a steadily encouraging voice for me as a writer.

Walaa

I believe that love is the only solution to our problems. I'm in love with being an English teacher for naughty smiley kids in Gaza, Palestine. I'm living a great journey of love with my remarkable and stunning husband, crowned with the presence of our little angle "Emma."

—One of my earliest conversations with Walaa addressed these questions: "What is love? Is love rational, or is it irrational? Does love endure, or does it fade?" I believe we agreed upon an answer

to the first question that embraced all of humanity—and all of the rowdy little boys she has taught in school. And if I recall correctly, we might summarize our long, complex answer to the second and third questions with a simple "yes." I have listened to Walaa speak with great compassion about her husband and her students, and about her deep desire to be a loving teacher and mother. She is.

About the Author

Kevin Hadduck recently retired from his academic career, but is still hiking, building/crafting things, and writing. His favorite part-time retirement job so far has been working for the college facilities crew, cleaning up large attics in campus buildings, shoveling snow, and keeping campus gardens. "I work alone," he says. "It's good therapy."

Other books by Kevin Hadduck

When Words Get In the Way, A Journey with Aphasia, Elaine Schultz and Kevin Hadduck, Stillwater Press, 2022

A Farewell to Lent, Cherry Grove Collections, Word Tech Communications, Cincinnati, Ohio, 2018.

Hymnody of the Blue Heron, Cherry Grove Collections, Word Tech Communications, Cincinnati, Ohio, 2016.

Fomite

Writing a review on social media sites for readers will help the progress of independent publishing. To submit a review, go to the book page on any of the sites and follow the links for reviews. Books from independent presses rely on reader-to-reader communications.

For more information or to order any of our books, visit:
http://www.fomitepress.com/our-books.html

More poetry from Fomite...

Fomite